www.cheekyprimate.com

Table of Content

Aurora

Auroras are beautiful displays of light that happen in the sky, usually near the North or South Pole where the sky gets really dark at night. These displays are caused by solar wind, made of tiny particles from the sun. When these particles hit the Earth's atmosphere, they create glowing colors such as green, pink, and purple.

Avalanche

Avalanches resemble giant snow slides and occur on mountains. When a steep slope becomes overloaded with snow, or if the weather changes rapidly, the snow can suddenly give way, hurtling down the mountainside at high speed. Avalanches are incredibly powerful and can be extremely dangerous, particularly during the snowy season.

Bioluminescence

Did you know that some animals in the ocean can make their own light? The superpower that makes these tiny creatures glow like stars in the water is called *Bioluminescence*. These special ocean animals, like jellyfish and tiny plankton, can make their light, like little flashlights built inside them! They use this light to find food, communicate with one another, and even scare predators away.

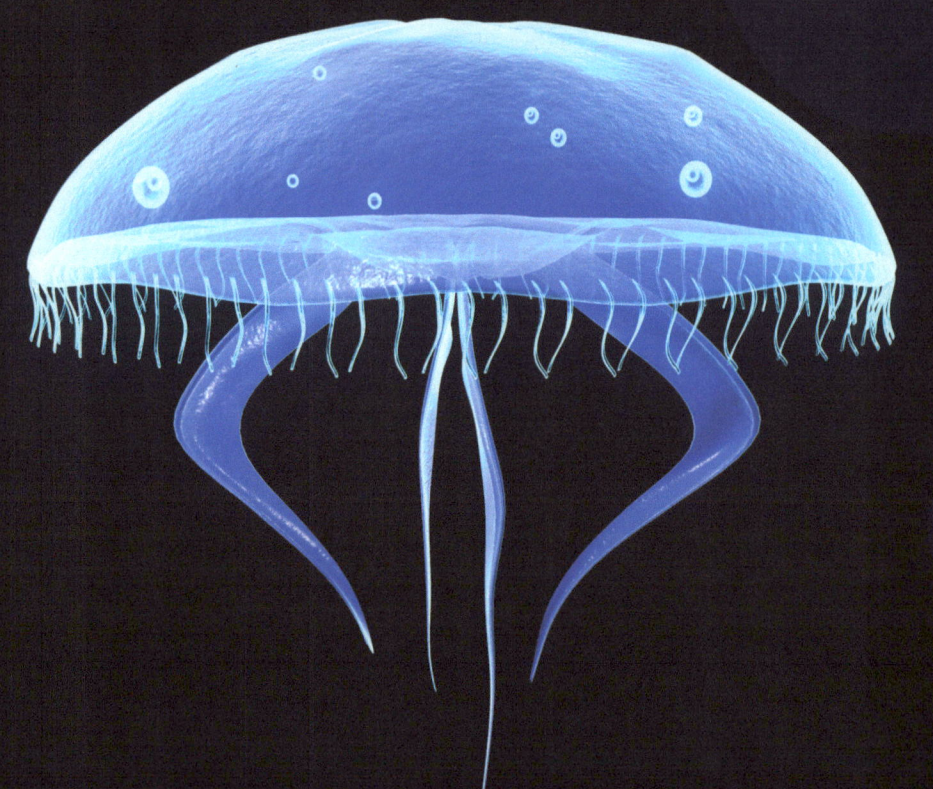

Cloud

Clouds look like fluffy, floating pillows in the sky. They're made up of tiny drops of water or ice crystals that come together high up in the air, forming different shapes and sizes. Clouds are important because they help determine the weather. When there are lots of clouds, it might rain or snow, but when there are no clouds, it's usually sunny.

Cross Pollination

Cross-pollination is a fascinating process that happens in plants to help them make seeds and grow into new plants. Flowers have a powdery substance called pollen inside them. When bees or butterflies visit one flower and then fly to another flower of the same kind, they carry pollen with them. This helps the flowers make seeds so new plants can grow.

Hummingbirds are also cross-pollinators! With their long, thin beaks and special tongues, they dive deep into flowers to sip nectar. As they do, they often brush against the flower's reproductive parts, picking up pollen and carrying it to other flowers.

Drought

Drought happens when there is low rainfall in an area for a long period of time. This can cause the land to be very dry and create problems for plants, animals, and people due to the lack of water. Farmers might face difficulties growing food, and rivers and lakes can dry up.

Desertification

Desertification is when once fertile land gradually becomes dry and barren, similar to a desert. This happens because of factors such as climate change, overgrazing by animals, and cutting down too many trees. When this happens, the soil and plants lose their ability to support life, making it hard for plants, animals, and people to live there.

Erosion

Erosion is nature's way of reshaping the Earth's surface over a long time. It happens when wind, water, or ice slowly wears away the soil and rocks on the land. Sometimes, erosion creates valleys, canyons, and beaches, but it can also cause problems by washing away soil that plants need to grow.

Earthquake

An earthquake is a big shake or rumble in the ground that happens when pieces of the Earth's surface, called 'Tectonic Plates,' suddenly move against each other. This movement creates powerful vibrations that make the ground shake. Earthquakes can cause buildings, trees, and even the ground to shake or move.

Fog

Fog is formed when cold air comes into contact with warmer ground or water. As the warm air cools down quickly, tiny water droplets form in the air, creating a thick mist that wraps around everything.

Flooding

Flooding happens when there's too much water in a place. This usually happens after heavy rain or when rivers overflow. When the ground can't soak up any more water, it starts to spread out, covering roads, fields, and sometimes even houses.

Germination

Germination is the exciting start of a plant's journey. It begins when a seed receives the right amount of water, warmth, and air, and starts to sprout. First, a tiny root stretches out into the soil, searching for food and water. Then, a little shoot pushes upwards, reaching for the sun until it becomes a young plant.

Hurricane

A hurricane is a powerful storm that forms over the warm ocean. It begins when thunderstorms gather strength and spin with the Earth's rotation. As the storm grows, it creates a special calm area called '*The Eye*' in the middle of the hurricane, surrounded by large rain clouds and strong winds that can cause damage to houses, trees, roads, and bridges.

Hibernation

Hibernation is the long nap that some animals take during the winter. When it gets cold and food becomes scarce, these animals find a cozy spot, like a burrow or a den, and snuggle up for a long sleep. During hibernation, their body temperature drops, and they breathe very slowly. This helps them save energy until it's warmer and food is more available again. Animals like bears, hedgehogs, and some frogs hibernate to survive the winter without having to eat too much.

Honey

Honey is a sweet treat made by bees. They collect nectar from flowers using their long tongues and store it in a special part of their bodies called the '*Honey Stomach*.' When they return to the hive, they share the nectar with other bees by regurgitating it into their mouths. Inside the hive, bees work together to turn the nectar into honey. They fan their wings to dry out the extra water, leaving behind the sticky and delicious honey stored in honeycombs.

17

Iceberg

Icebergs are huge chunks of ice that break off from glaciers and float in the ocean. They can be found in different sizes, with some as tall as skyscrapers! Even though you only see a little bit above the water, most of the iceberg is hiding underneath, which makes them a hidden danger for ships sailing in icy waters.

Jet Stream

Picture a super-fast wind highway high in the sky. That's the jet stream! Formed by differences in temperature between warm and cold air as the Earth rotates, this powerful wind helps move weather all around the world. Pilots also take advantage of its power to fly faster and save fuel when they're traveling in the same direction as the jet stream.

Kettle Lake

A kettle lake is formed when a big chunk of ice from a melting glacier gets buried in the ground. After the ice melts away, it leaves a hole behind, which fills up with water to create the lake. These lakes are often small and shallow and can be found in places where glaciers used to be, like parts of North America and Europe. They provide a habitat for different types of plants and animals.

Lightning

Lightning is a powerful spark of electricity that occurs when clouds become charged with electricity during thunderstorms. When these charges build up, they create a giant spark between the clouds or between the clouds and the ground, sometimes causing damage to buildings and trees. Lightning is incredibly hot and can reach temperatures hotter than the surface of the sun.

<u>M</u>etamorphosis

Metamorphosis is a transformation some animals go through as they grow up. For example, butterflies start as tiny eggs, then hatch into caterpillars, also called *larvae*. These caterpillars eat and grow until they form a protective casing called the *chrysalis* around themselves before they transform into adult butterflies. This transformation helps them adapt to different environments at different stages of their growth.

While inside the chrysalis, the caterpillar's body undergoes a fascinating process called *Histolysis*, where it is broken down into a soup-like substance. From this mixture, the tissues and organs of the adult butterfly gradually form, completing its remarkable transformation.

Migration

Migration is when animals travel from one place to another at certain times of the year. They do this to find food, have babies, or escape cold weather. Birds, such as geese and ducks, fly to warmer places in the winter and return home when it gets warmer. Other animals that also migrate include whales and butterflies.

Geese can travel thousands of miles during migration, often communicating with each other by honking loudly while flying in a V-shaped formation to save energy.

Natural Springs

Natural springs are spots where groundwater bubbles up to the Earth's surface. Groundwater forms when rain or melted snow seeps underground and collects in big storage areas called *aquifers*. When enough pressure builds up, the water rises back up, creating a spring! Springs are often found in valleys or at the base of mountains. Some burst out like waterfalls, while others trickle gently.

Ocean Tide

Ocean tides are the rising and falling of the sea that happens approximately twice every day. They're caused by the moon's gravity pulling on the water as the Earth rotates. When the moon is above, it pulls the water towards it, creating a *high tide*. And when it's not, the water bulges out on the opposite side, also creating a high tide. In between these two high tides are areas where water levels are lower, known as *low tides*. The sun's gravity also plays a part, making some tides higher than others.

Photosynthesis

Photosynthesis is how plants make their food using sunlight, water, and carbon dioxide from the air. They use sunlight to turn water and carbon dioxide into glucose, which gives them energy to grow. Plus, they release oxygen into the air as a part of this process, which is essential for living things to breathe.

Quicksand

Quicksand is a mixture of sand, clay, and water that forms a thick, fluid-like substance. It often looks like ordinary sand but can be dangerous because it acts like a liquid, making it difficult for objects or people to escape if they become trapped in it. Despite its name, quicksand doesn't actually pull people under like in movies; most people float on its surface due to its lower density. Nevertheless, it can still be challenging to escape without help.

Rainbow

Rainbows happen when sunlight shines through raindrops in the air. Each tiny drop acts like a mini *prism*, bending the light and splitting it into different colors. When many raindrops do this together, a beautiful arc of colors stretches across the sky. The colors in a rainbow are red, orange, yellow, green, blue, indigo, and violet, and they always appear in that order.

Solar Eclipse

A solar eclipse happens when the moon moves between the sun and the Earth, blocking sunlight and casting a shadow on the Earth. It can be total, where the sky darkens as if it were nighttime, partial, or annular, depending on how much of the sun is covered. It's essential to wear proper eye protection when viewing a solar eclipse to protect your eyes from the sun's harmful rays.

Sunrise

A sunrise is a daily event that marks the beginning of a new day. As the Earth rotates, different parts of the planet gradually receive the light from the sun's rays, making it look like the sun is rising. The colors of a sunrise can change depending on the weather and the particles in the air!

Sunset

A sunset happens when the sun goes down below the horizon, marking the end of daylight. As the Earth spins on its axis, different parts of the planet experience sunset at different times depending on where they are relative to the sun. During a sunset, the sky gradually turns from light to dark as the sun's rays fade away.

Tectonic Plates

Tectonic plates are huge pieces of the Earth's outer shell that fit together like a jigsaw puzzle. They float on a layer underneath and are always moving, even though we can't feel it. Sometimes, when these plates bump into each other or slide past each other, they can cause earthquakes, volcanoes, and mountains to form.

Tornado

A tornado forms during severe thunderstorms when warm, moist air rises and meets cooler, drier air. This clash creates a swirling column of air that extends to the ground. As the rotating air gets stronger, it can turn into a tornado, usually accompanied by severe weather such as strong winds, hail, and heavy rain. Tornadoes typically don't last long, but they can be extremely destructive to everything in their path, making them one of the most dangerous things in nature.

Tsunami

A tsunami is a series of powerful ocean waves caused by underwater earthquakes, volcanic eruptions, or landslides. These events displace large volumes of water, creating massive waves that can travel across the ocean at high speeds. When a tsunami approaches shallow areas, the waves can increase in height and become extremely destructive by flooding everything in their path.

Upwelling

Upwelling is a process where cold, nutrient-rich water from the depths of the ocean rises to the surface. It typically occurs along coastlines when winds push surface water away from the shore, allowing the colder water below to replace it. This cold water is packed with nutrients, which support the growth of tiny plants called *phytoplankton*. The abundance of nutrients during upwelling also attracts other marine creatures such as fish and seabirds.

V̲olcano

Volcanoes are openings in the Earth's crust where magma, gases, and ash can escape from deep below the surface. They form when magma, which is molten rock, rises and erupts onto the land or into the ocean, releasing lava flows, ash clouds, and gases. While volcanic eruptions pose risks to nearby areas, volcanoes also shape the Earth's surface and provide essential nutrients for soil and plant growth.

Wildfire

A wildfire is an uncontrolled fire that spreads rapidly through vegetation, such as forests, grasslands, or brush. These fires can start naturally from lightning strikes or human activities like campfires. When the weather is dry and windy, wildfires can quickly grow out of control, destroying everything in their path. They also release large amounts of smoke, ash, and heat, which can be harmful to people, wildlife, and property.

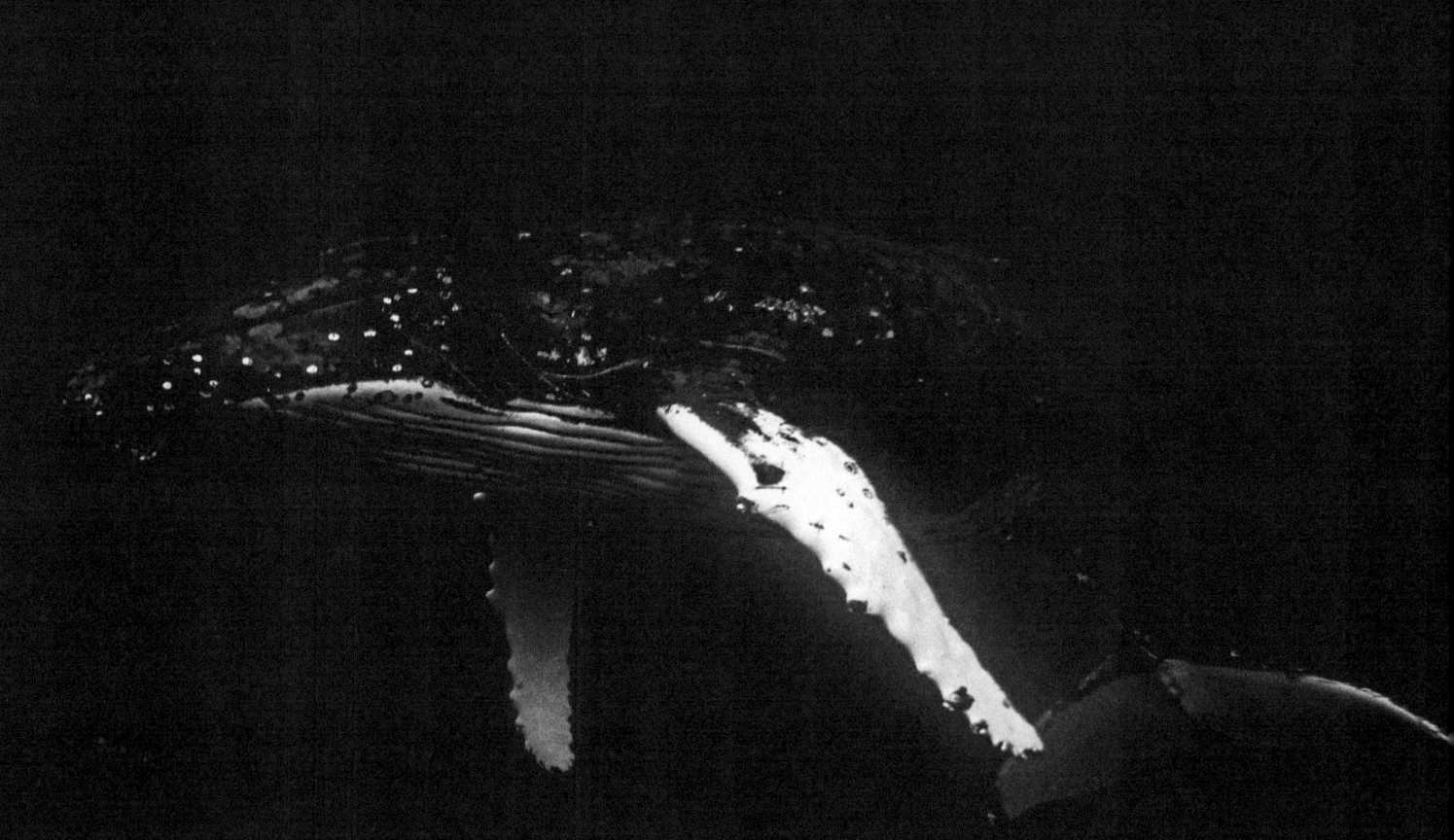

Whale Fall

A whale fall occurs when a dead whale sinks to the ocean floor, providing a sudden and massive source of nutrients to deep-sea ecosystems. As the whale carcass decomposes, it attracts scavengers such as sharks and hagfish, along with other smaller marine creatures and bacteria. Once the flesh has been consumed, bone-eating worms break down the remaining bones, recycling nutrients within the deep-sea environment.

Xenoliths

Xenoliths are pieces of rock found within volcanic rocks. They form when hot magma from deep within the Earth's crust carries pieces of surrounding rocks to the surface during volcanic eruptions. These "guest rocks" get trapped in the cooling magma and become part of the volcanic rock.

41

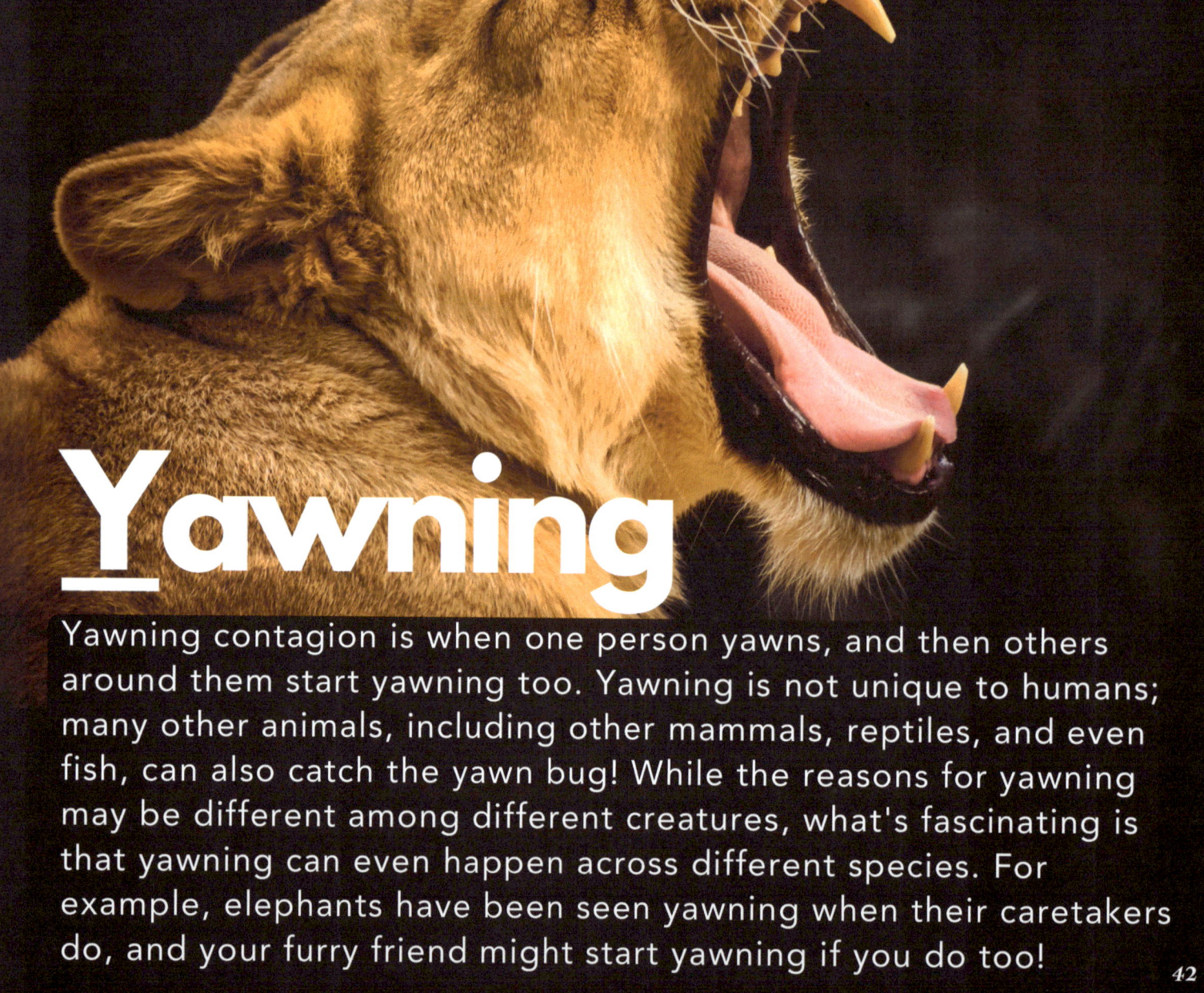

Yawning

Yawning contagion is when one person yawns, and then others around them start yawning too. Yawning is not unique to humans; many other animals, including other mammals, reptiles, and even fish, can also catch the yawn bug! While the reasons for yawning may be different among different creatures, what's fascinating is that yawning can even happen across different species. For example, elephants have been seen yawning when their caretakers do, and your furry friend might start yawning if you do too!

Zonal Wind

Zonal winds play an important role in shaping our global climate and weather systems. They are crucial for distributing heat and moisture around the planet, which influences weather patterns and ocean currents. Depending on the location and season, zonal winds can either blow from west to east or from east to west.

Share Your Thoughts!

Your opinion is incredibly valuable to me, and I would be thrilled if you could leave a review. Also, don't forget to scan the QR code to stay connected for more exciting content and updates!

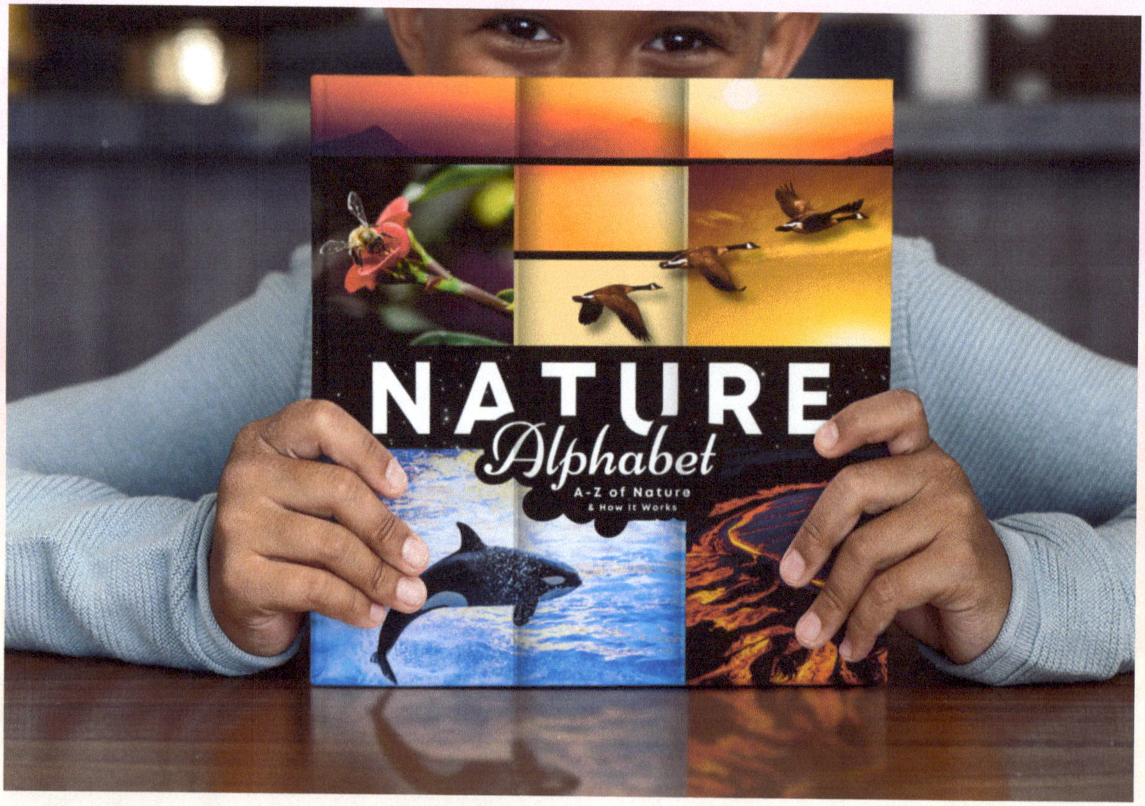

More From Cheekyprimate

The Ultimate Volcano Guide

Is your child fascinated by volcanoes? With its easy-to-follow language, stunning visuals, interactive activities, and engaging quizzes, this book is the perfect way for kids to explore the exciting world of volcanoes.

Get ready to become an animal facts champion!

Did you know sharks have a secret stash of teeth and octopuses are multitasking masters with 3 hearts and 8 brains? This comprehensive animal encyclopedia is filled with over 100 fascinating facts from ecosystems around the world.

Store

Scan the QR code above to visit my bookstore and stay connected for more updates on my projects!

Learning is fun!